TITLE: Store it!

AUTHOR: Henry Pluckrose

SERIES: Ways to...

PUBLICATION DATE: MARCH, 1990

ISBN: 0-531-14021-0

GRADES: K-4

BINDING: REINFORCED LIBRARY BINDING

PRICE: $10.40

PAGES: 32

BRIEF DESCRIPTION:

This book examines different ways to say "store it."

387 Park Avenue South, New York, N.Y. 10016

Franklin Watts Inc.
387 Park Avenue South
New York, N.Y. 10016

Library of Congress Cataloging-in-Publication Data
Pluckrose, Henry Arthur.
Store it! / by Henry Pluckrose.
p. cm. — (Ways to)
Includes index.
Summary: Color photos and simple text explore different ways of saying "Store it!."
ISBN 0-531-14021-0
1. Vocabulary—Juvenile literature. [1. Vocabulary.] I. Title.
II. Series: Pluckrose, Henry Arthur. Ways to.
PE1449.P58 1989
428.1—dc20 89-5823
CIP
AC

Editor: Ruth Thomson
Design: K & Co

Printed in Italy by
G. Canale S.p.A., Turin

Ways to....

STORE *it!*

Henry Pluckrose

Photography by Chris Fairclough

FRANKLIN WATTS

London • New York • Sydney • Toronto

Think how many ways there are of storing things.

Cans and bags, bottles and boxes, tins and cartons come in different shapes and sizes. Have you ever wondered why?

What's wrong here? What sort of containers do we usually use for these things?

We keep these foods in jars and tins. We can open and close the jars and tins to use their contents every day.

A can looks like a tin but its top does not open and close. When you open it, you must eat the food right away.

We keep all sorts of other things in jars and tins.
The lids keep the contents airtight and stop them from changing.

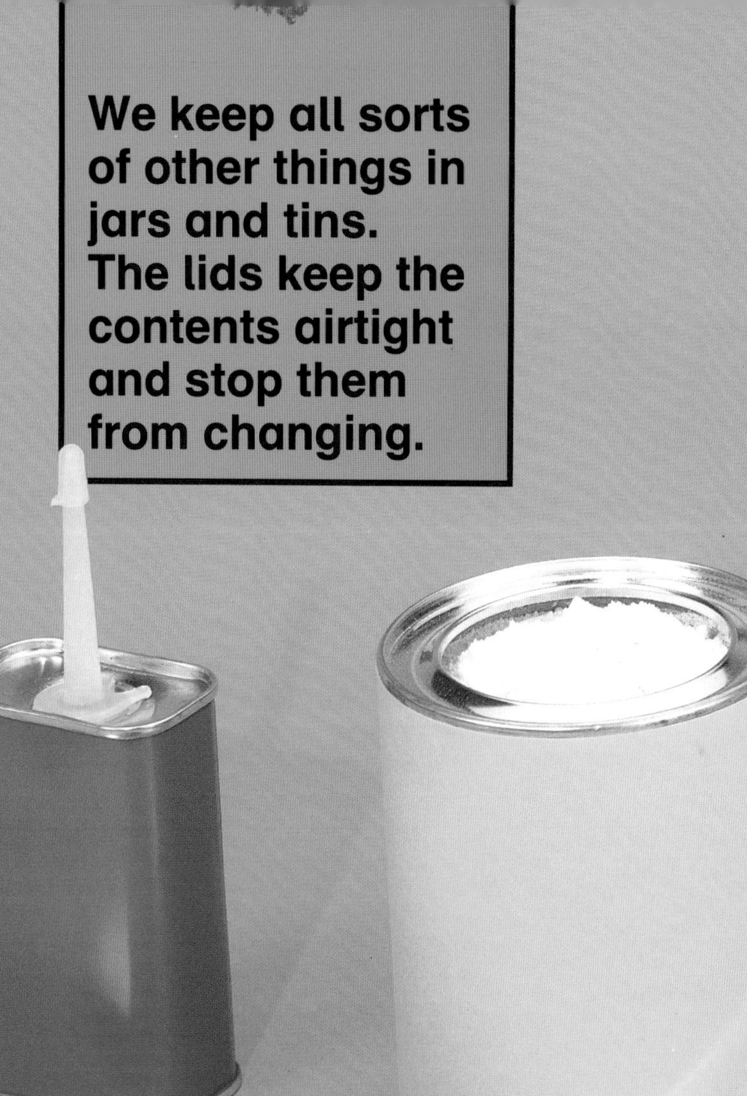

We often keep liquids in bottles. The shape of the bottle helps us to pour the liquid easily.

Why does a perfume bottle have a smaller hole than a drink bottle?

Some liquids are too thick to pour. They are kept in tubes instead of bottles. How do you get them out?

Dry things are often kept in boxes, but never baked beans!

We keep jewels in a jewel box. We store tools in a tool box. We put a first aid kit in a case which keeps it clean.

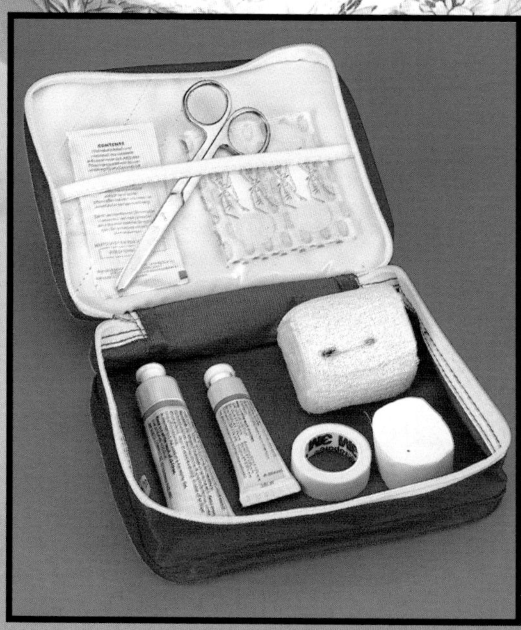

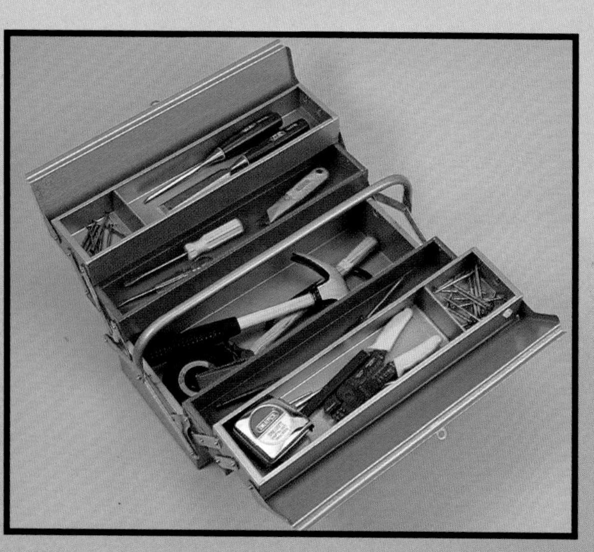

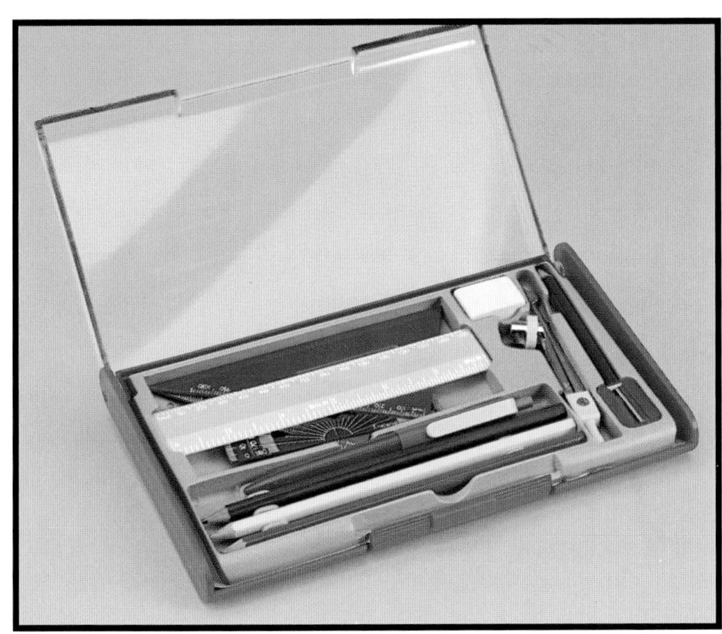

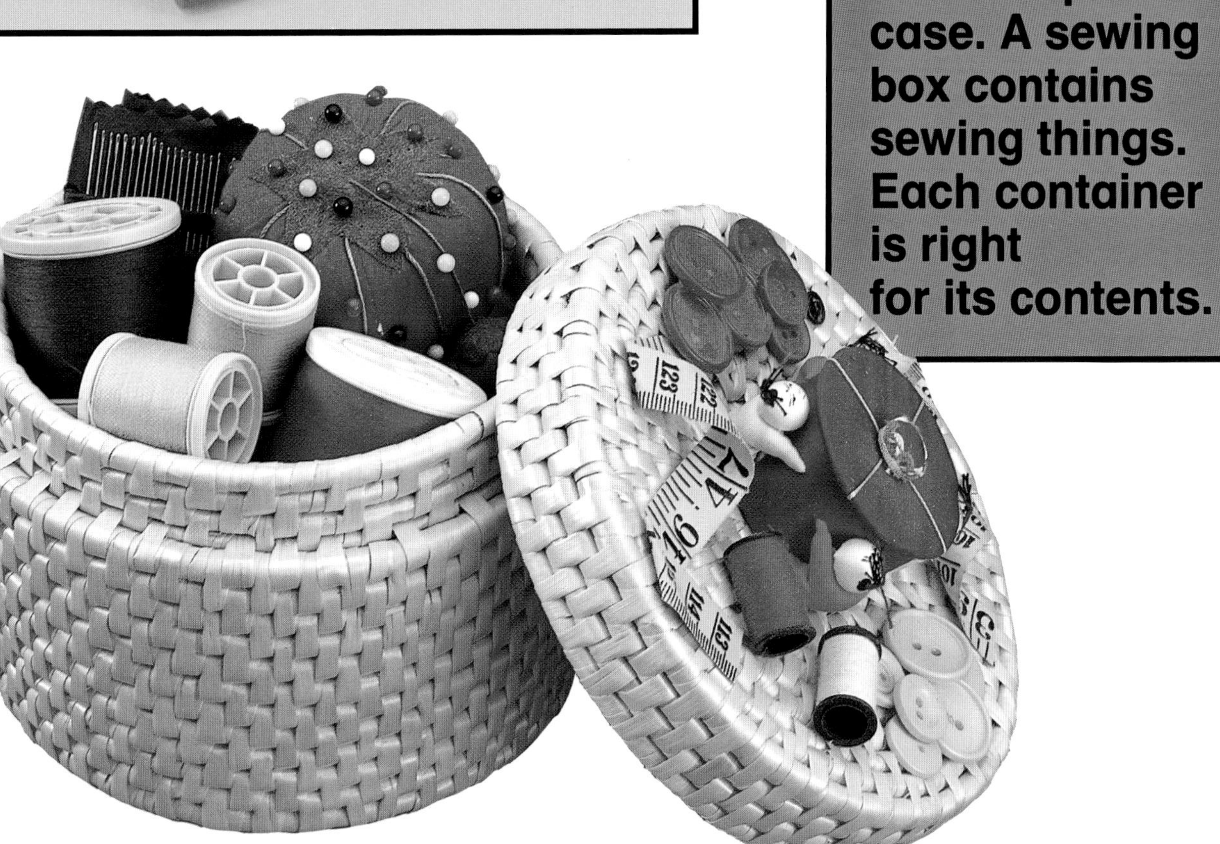

Pens and pencils fit into a pencil case. A sewing box contains sewing things. Each container is right for its contents.

We could put all these things in a bag.

Why has the bag changed shape?

We keep clothes in a closet or a chest of drawers. When we travel we put them in a suitcase.

We keep money in a wallet or a purse.
Why don't we keep it in a paper bag or an old sock?

Can you match these things with their containers?

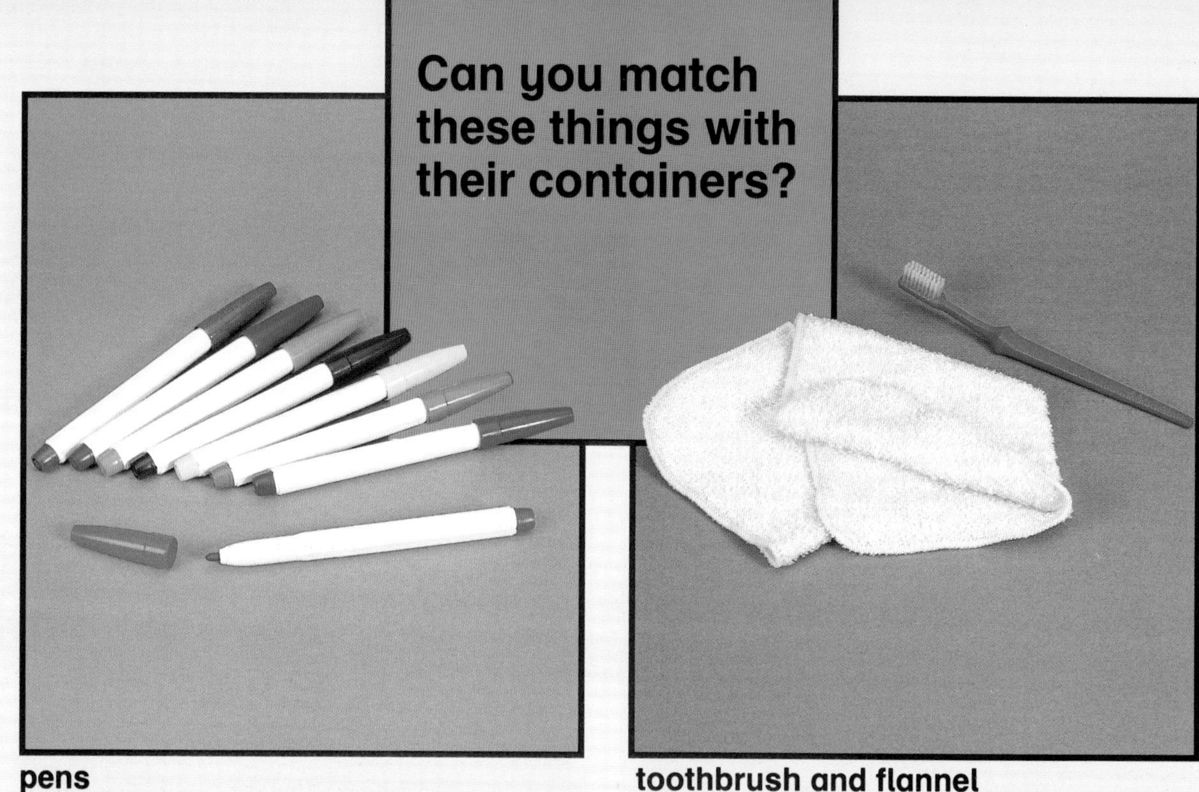

pens

toothbrush and flannel

dominoes

beads

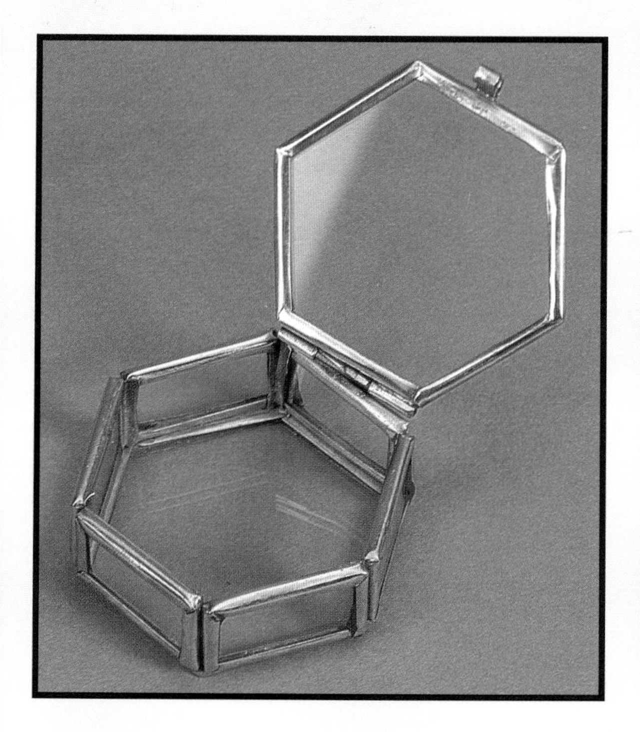
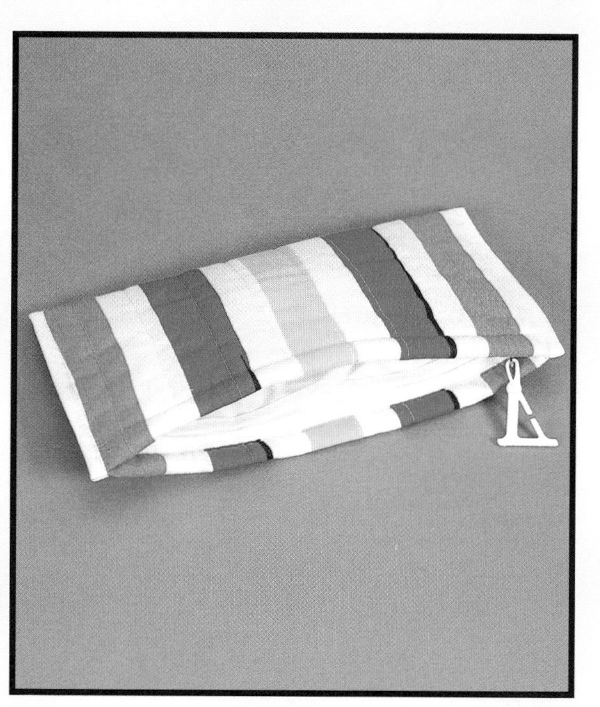

There are many other ways of storing things. Can you guess what each of these containers holds?

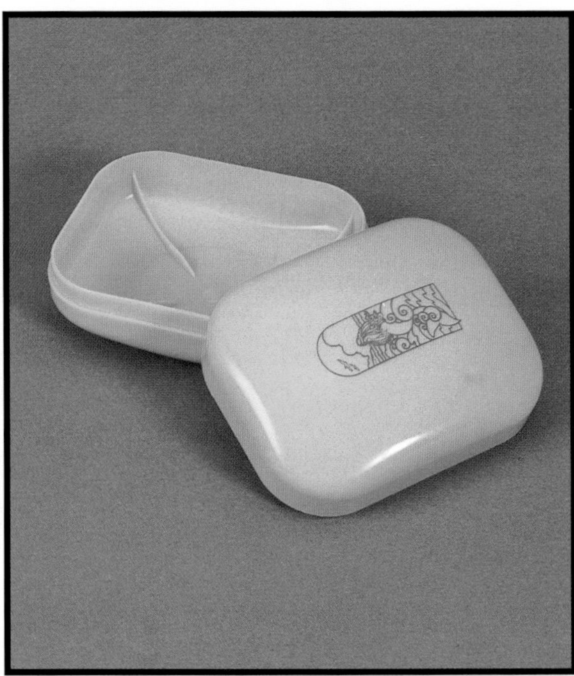

D
COUNT
DUCKULA

Things to do

- **Sand, water and vegetables**

Try this experiment out of doors

Collect these containers:

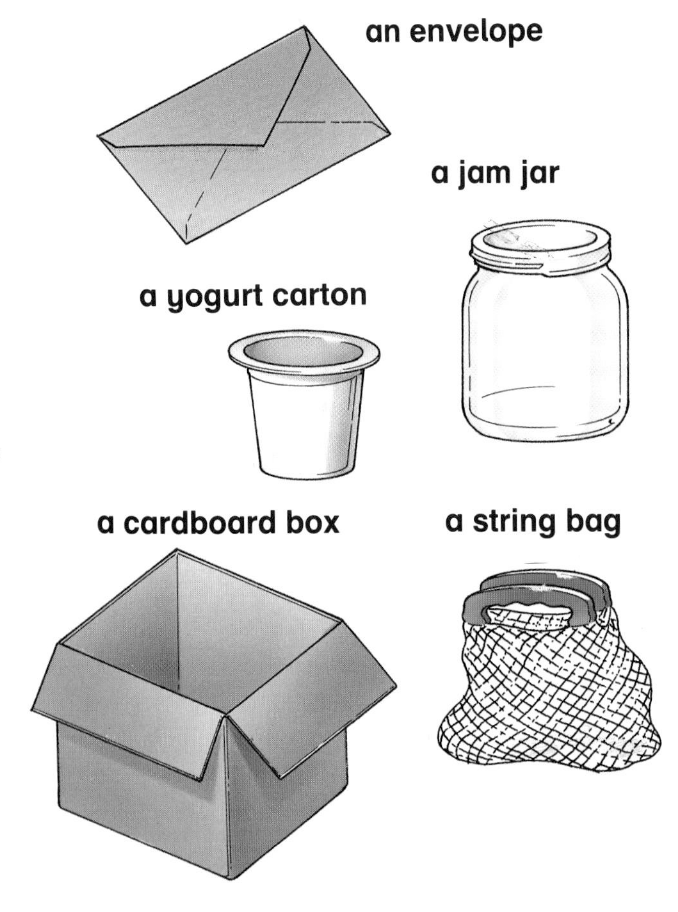

Fill each one with sand. Which of them are suitable for holding sand? Which are useless?

Now fill the same things with water. Which containers hold water well? Which of them will hold water for only a short time?

Now try filling each container with some carrots, onions or potatoes. Which containers are most suitable for holding large, odd-shaped vegetables? Which are quite unsuitable?

• Can you find...?

Think hard and look around you to find...

- 10 different ways in which we store food.
- 5 different kinds of places in which we keep clothes.
- 5 different places in which we keep important papers.
- 10 different containers in which we keep liquids.
- 5 different ways in which we store tools.
- 5 different kinds of containers for storing medicines and ointments.
- 5 different ways of keeping money safely in one place.

• Storage places

Choose one place, for example the room you are in or your parents' car. See how many places there are in it for storing things safely and conveniently.

Words about storing

hold
keep
pack
place
preserve
stack

Storage containers

bag
basket
beaker
bin
bottle
bucket
can
case
carton
chest
churn
compartment
cupboard
drawer
envelope
file
folder
flask
holdall
jar
money box
packet
packing case
pot
purse
pack
safe
shelf
suitcase
tin
tray
trunk
tube
wallet

Pluckrose, Henry. *Move It!*; ISBN 0-531-14020-2. *Store It!*; ISBN 0-531-14021-0. Each book: illus. with photographs by Chris Fairclough. Watts, 1990. 32p. (Ways to . . . Books). $10.40.

Ad *4-6 yrs.* Although the backcover copy ("Each book focuses on a particular action verb . . .") appears to have been written by someone who hasn't read the books, these, like *Cut It!* and *Join It!* (BCCB 2/90) are crisply designed introductions to basic physical concepts. *Move It!* provides an unenlightening definition of gravity ("Our planet earth pulls everything toward it") but further pages on wheels and wind and power are clear and accompanied by exemplary color photos. *Store It!*, about containers, is also sometimes conceptually fuzzy ("The lids keep the contents airtight and stop them from changing") but features some intriguing questions ("Why does a perfume bottle have a smaller hole than a drink bottle?") and guessing games ("Can you match these things with their containers?"). Both books include some rather weak suggestions for further projects; prefer in-action enactments of the demonstrations mentioned above. RS
D.V. Everyday life concepts